MEXICO

Susan Canizares • Pamela Chanko

Scholastic Inc.
New York • Toronto • London • Auckland • Sydney

Acknowledgments

Literacy Specialist: Linda Cornwell

Social Studies Consultant: Barbara Schubert, Ph.D.

Design: Silver Editions

Photo Research: Silver Editions

Endnotes: Jacqueline Smith

Endnote Illustrations: Anthony Carnabucia

Photographs: Cover: Robert Frerck/Tony Stone Images; p. 1: Eric A. Wessman/The Viesti Collection; p. 2: B. Daemmrich/The Image Works; p. 3: Jean-Marc Giboux/Gamma Liaison; p. 4: Marco/The Viesti Collection; p. 5: B. Daemmrich/Stock Boston; p. 6: Bill Schildge/Pacific Stock; p. 7: Cosmo Condina/Tony Stone Images; p. 8: Joseph F. Viesti/The Viesti Collection; p. 9: Cliff Hollenbeck/International Stock; pp. 10, 11: Robert Frerck/Tony Stone Images; p. 12: Tibor Bognar/The Stock Market.

Library of Congress Cataloging-in-Publication Data
Canizares, Susan 1960-
Mexico/Susan Canizares, Pamela Chanko.
p.cm. -- (Social studies emergent readers)
Summary: Simple text and photographs present people in Mexico playing music and soccer, working, shopping, dancing, fishing, and farming.
ISBN 0-439-04570-3 (pbk.: alk. paper)
1. Mexico--Description and travel--Juvenile literature.
2. Country life--Mexico--Juvenile literature. [1. Mexico--Social life and customs.] I. Chanko, Pamela, 1968-. II. Title. III. Series.
F1216.5.C36 1999

972--dc21   98-53355
                                                                        CIP AC

10   08   09 08 07 06 05 04

Living in Mexico.

Reading

and writing.

Playing music

and playing soccer.

Working

and shopping.

Dressing up

and dancing.

Fishing

and farming.

Mexico.

MEXICO

Mexico is part of North America and connects the continent to Central and South America. Spanish is the official language because Mexico was a Spanish colony for a long time. Mexico is a heavily populated country—in fact, Mexico City, the capital, is the most populated city in the world.

Reading and writing About 100 years ago, schools in Mexico were not free for all children. Only one in four Mexicans could read and write. The government decided that something had to be done about it and slowly started building more schools and training teachers. Now free education is available for everyone and almost 90% of the people can read and write.

Music and soccer These children are playing music at a fiesta—a holiday celebration—for Mexico's Independence Day, September 16. Mexico has a rich and varied music tradition. The ancient music of the many tribes of Mexican Indians who first inhabited Mexico was played on gourd rattles, shells, drums and flutes, and can still be heard in parts of Mexico. Corridos are a popular kind of folk song, with their stories of bandits, sheriffs, and the Mexican Revolution. Most famous are the strolling mariachi bands of singers, guitars, trumpets, and violins that play on streets and in cafes.

Soccer is the most popular sport in Mexico. People in Mexico often start up soccer games in empty fields or lots. There are many amateur teams, and the professional soccer leagues have produced some excellent players over the years.

Working and shopping Pottery is one of the most ancient crafts in Mexico. Clay figurines dating back to 12,000 B.C. have been found there. Skilled craftspeople in Mexico have always made colorful ceramic water jugs, pots, dishes, jewelry, and even instruments like flutes and rattles. In parts of Mexico, people make these objects by hand and sell them for a living.

Many Mexicans shop for their fresh food at open-air markets. These markets sell many of the same fruits and vegetables you may find in outdoor markets in your town, but there are also many tropical fruits like mangoes, papayas, and avocados. Many of the stalls are filled with chili peppers in all different colors and shapes. There are over 100 varieties in Mexico!

Dressing up and dancing For some holidays and other special occasions, Mexicans wear traditional national costumes. For men this usually means tight deerskin or velvet riding pants with gold or silver buttons down the sides, a short bolero jacket, a big red bow tie, spurred boots, and a big white sombrero. Women's costumes vary from place to place but the most common is the china poblana—a full red and green skirt decorated with beads, a brightly embroidered short-sleeved blouse, and a bright sash.

Dancing is very popular in Mexico, and each region has dozens of folk dances that are performed on special occasions. Since ancient times, Mexican Indians have dressed up and danced to bring luck in war, marriage, hunting, and the harvest. Many of these dances, like the deer dance, are still performed today. The most famous of these is the Mexican hat dance, with its fast hopping and heel tapping.

Fishing and farming The Tarascan Indians still fish from their dugout canoes, using traditional butterfly nets. The waters near Mexico and California teem with shrimp, anchovies, oysters, sardines, and tuna. But Mexicans do not eat a lot of fish and only started fishing commercially in the last few decades.

The situation with farming is exactly the opposite. Many people try to make a living by farming. However, suitable land for growing crops is diminishing. Mexico's main crop is corn, but it is also a big producer of bananas, beans, coffee, cotton, oranges, and tropical fruits.

Flag The Mexican flag is a tricolore (tri = three; colore = color) with its green, white, and red stripes. In the center is an emblem showing an old Aztec myth about the founding of Mexico. The Aztec prophets believed that they should settle down in the place where they saw eagle perched on a cactus and eating a snake. They found that place in Mexico.